CIRCULATING WITH THE LISTED PROBLEM(S):

Scribbles   2-7-18 HS

World Crafts and Recipes

Recipe and Craft Guide to

CHINA

Joanne Mattern

Mitchell Lane

P.O. Box 196
Hockessin, Delaware 19707
Visit us on the web: www.mitchelllane.com
Comments? email us: mitchelllane@mitchelllane.com

Mitchell Lane
PUBLISHERS

World Crafts and Recipes

The Caribbean • China • France • India • Indonesia • Japan

Library of Congress Cataloging-in-Publication Data

Mattern, Joanne, 1963–
  Recipe and craft guide to China / by Joanne Mattern.
    p. cm. — (World crafts and recipes)
  Includes bibliographical references and index.
  ISBN 978-1-58415-937-7 (library bound)
  1. Cookery, Chinese—Juvenile literature. 2. Handicraft—China—Juvenile literature. I. Title.
TX724.5.C5M352 2010
  641.591—dc22
                                    2010009242

Printing 1 2 3 4 5 6 7 8 9

PLB

CONTENTS

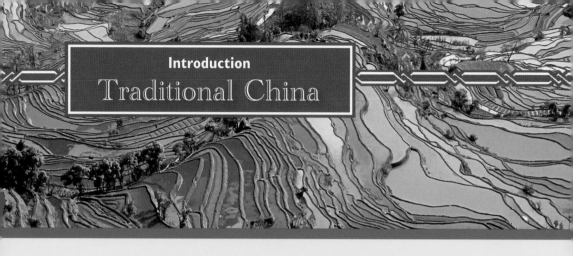

China is a huge country in Asia—about the same size as the United States—and people have lived there for thousands of years. Since it covers such a large area (3.7 million square miles, or 9.6 million square kilometers), its climate varies greatly, from the snow-capped Himalayas in the north to the rainy plains where rice is grown, to the balmy beaches on the South China Sea. More than 1.3 billion people live in China, and Shanghai and Beijing are two of the most populated cities in the world.

With the variation in climate comes variety in cuisine. While rice is the main food in the southern part of the country, in the north, where winters are freezing and summers hot, the people enjoy noodle and pancake dishes as well. Meat is more prevalent in northern Sichuan, but vegetables are a major part of meals across the country.

In the province of Sichuan, which was along the ancient trade route called the Silk Road, spicier foods evolved. There, chilies, Sichuan peppercorns, garlic, and onions give food some extra fire.

Traditional Chinese cooking does not use as much processed food as American (or even Chinese-American) cooking does. Sweet desserts, such as cookies, candy, or cake, are not common, either—although some recipes from eastern China do call for sugar. Instead of sweets, the Chinese often eat fruit at the end of their meal.

The Chinese honor tradition, which is evident in their cuisine and their art. Chinese art often includes animal images and creatures such as the dragon, which are important parts of the nation's folklore. The dragon is especially powerful, as it is an ancient symbol of strength and wisdom.

I first became interested in China in 1999, when my husband and I adopted a baby girl from that country. Our adoption trip included two weeks in China, and our family was able to explore different parts of the country and see many examples of the beautiful art and culture there. We

also enjoyed many delicious Chinese meals that were nothing like the Americanized food we'd eaten at Chinese restaurants at home! By 2007, our family had grown to include three more Chinese children, and we experienced three more fascinating and delightful trips to China. Since then, our family has incorporated Chinese cooking and traditions into our daily lives. It is my pleasure to share some of these foods and crafts with you, so you can enjoy China's charm as much as we do.

Although there are large supermarkets in China's major cities, many Chinese people prefer to shop in smaller local stores, which have a surprising variety of products. Groceries are usually kept behind counters, and customers ask for the items they want. The clerk writes out a slip listing the items and the prices. When the customer is finished, he or she takes the slip to a main cashier and pays for the items.

Fresh food is important to Chinese cooks. Many people in China shop at wet markets. A wet market is like a huge farmer's market and can be located either outside or inside. Different vendors set up stands or tables and sell fresh fruit, vegetables, spices, meat, and fish. Customers can pick exactly what they want because all the food is set out and available for touching and squeezing. Customers can also scoop out and buy rice from huge bags or purchase freshly made noodles.

Buying fish and meat in a wet market is a very different experience than buying these items in an American grocery store. The fish and meat in a wet market are not neatly packaged the way they are in the United States. Instead, the customer chooses the live fish, chicken, duck, or other animal he or she wants, and a worker slaughters it on site. Although this might be upsetting to some people, it insures that the food is extremely fresh. Wet markets also sell foods that are not normally seen in American supermarkets, such as frog and eel. If you live near or travel to a large American city that includes a Chinatown, you can experience the sights and sounds of an open-air market very similar to the wet markets in China.

People in China might shop every day or several times a week in order to get the freshest foods. Smaller trips also help with food storage, as most Chinese homes and apartments are very small and do not have large pantries or freezers where food can be stored for long periods of time.

Many of the ingredients for the recipes in this book can be found in large supermarkets, in the international section. Other ingredients can be purchased at international or Asian grocery stores or online.

NOTE: Be sure to have an adult help you with dangerous cooking chores, such as using the oven or chopping or cutting with a knife. Many Chinese recipes use hot oil, which can splatter and burn you if you are not careful. It's best to have an adult work on these parts of the recipes.

White Rice

People have been growing rice in China for thousands of years. Southern China is perfectly suited for growing rice, which requires a hot, wet climate. Rice is also a healthy, filling food that goes well with most other foods. No meal in China is complete without bowls of steaming rice! This basic part of Chinese cooking is easy to make and a simple dish to start your cooking adventures.

Ingredients:

2 cups long-grain white rice
3 cups water

Instructions:

1. Pour the rice into a colander. Place the colander in the sink and run cold water over the rice while stirring gently. Rinse for one or two minutes until the water runs clear.
2. Drain the rice into a three-quart saucepan. Add water and bring it to a boil.
3. Reduce heat to low. Cover the saucepan and let the rice cook for 15-20 minutes, until all the water is absorbed.
4. Fluff the rice with a fork or chopsticks.
5. Place rice into bowls and serve. Serves 4 people.

Chicken and Pineapple Fried Rice

Many Chinese meals combine rice with meat, vegetables, and fruit. Fried rice is a quick and easy meal that can include many different ingredients.

Ingredients:

2 eggs
3 tablespoons vegetable oil
8 ounces cooked chicken breasts, sliced into 1-inch strips
½ cup chopped onion
4 cups cooked long-grain rice
8 ounces pineapple chunks
2 tablespoons soy sauce
2 tablespoons sliced almonds or cashew halves (optional)

Instructions:

1. Crack the eggs into a bowl. Beat the eggs lightly with a fork. Set aside.
2. **Have an adult** heat a wok over medium-high heat for about one minute. Pour the vegetable oil into the wok and heat for about 30 seconds.
3. Add chicken strips and onions to the wok. Stir-fry for about two minutes.
4. Add the rice and pineapple chunks and stir-fry for one to two minutes.
5. Cook the scrambled eggs in a separate pan. Add to the rice mixture.
6. Add soy sauce and stir-fry for another minute, mixing well.
7. Place your meal in a serving bowl. Top with almonds or cashews if you like. Serves 4 people.

BE SURE TO WASH YOUR HANDS AFTER TOUCHING RAW EGGS OR MEAT. YOU MUST ALSO WASH ANY SURFACES OR UTENSILS THAT CAME IN CONTACT WITH THE EGGS OR MEAT BEFORE IT WAS COOKED.

NOTE: You can also add other vegetables to this dish. Try peas, bell pepper strips, sliced carrots, or baby corn. You can also substitute pork, shrimp, or tofu for the chicken, or scallions along with or instead of onions.

Pork Lo Mein

Chinese noodles can be made of wheat, rice, or even bean paste. Noodles are more popular in the northern part of China because its cool, dry climate is more suited for growing wheat. Lo mein noodles are long and thin, like spaghetti. They can be paired with different meats and sauces.

Ingredients:

1 pound thin spaghetti or lo mein noodles
⅓ cup hoisin sauce
2 tablespoons soy sauce
1 tablespoon fresh ginger, chopped and grated OR 1 teaspoon powdered ginger
½ teaspoon cornstarch
3 teaspoons vegetable oil
8 ounces pork, sliced into one-inch strips
1 package (10-16 ounces) frozen mixed vegetables, such as carrots, broccoli, and cabbage
3 green onions, cut into one-inch pieces

Instructions:

1. Fill a saucepan with water and bring to a boil. Add noodles or spaghetti and cook for about 8-10 minutes, or until just soft. Drain into a colander and set aside.
2. Mix the hoisin sauce, soy sauce, ginger, and cornstarch in a bowl or cup until smooth. Set aside.
3. **Ask an adult** to heat vegetable oil in a wok or skillet over medium-high heat until hot. Add pork and cook for 3-4 minutes, until the meat is no longer pink.
4. Add vegetables and green onions and stir-fry until they are cooked but still crisp. Add the sauce mixture and heat until it boils.
5. Place noodles in a bowl and pour the meat and vegetable mixture on top. Stir to mix, and then serve. Serves 4 people.

Lo mein made with wheat noodles (above) and rice noodles (below).

Cold Sesame Noodles

Noodles are a mainstay at New Year's celebrations, because the long noodles symbolize a long life. This dish is often served at the beginning of a meal or as the main course during hot weather.

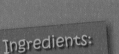

Ingredients:

1   pound thin spaghetti or lo mein noodles
3   tablespoons sesame oil
½ cup peanut butter
½ cup chicken broth or vegetable broth
3   tablespoons soy sauce
1   tablespoon sugar
¼ cup chopped peanuts or chopped green onions (optional)

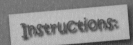

Instructions:

1. Fill a saucepan with water and bring to a boil. Add spaghetti and cook for about 8-10 minutes, or until just soft. **Ask an adult** to drain it with a colander. Add 1 tablespoon of sesame oil, mix, and set aside in the refrigerator for an hour.
2. Place peanut butter, broth, soy sauce, sesame oil, and sugar in a jar with a lid. Cover and shake well. Place in the refrigerator for about an hour.
3. Place the cold noodles on a serving dish. Top with peanut butter mixture and mix well.
4. Garnish with chopped peanuts or chopped green onions if you want to. Serves 4 people.

DUMPLINGS
Steamed Dumplings

Dumplings are eaten with everyday meals and also at holidays. They can include all sorts of fillings, including meat, shrimp, or vegetables. Chinese people enjoy dumplings by dipping them into sauce.

Ingredients:

3 cups Chinese cabbage (also called bok choy), finely chopped, rinsed, and drained
1 cup chopped scallions
1 pound ground pork
1 tablespoon fresh ginger, chopped and grated OR 1 teaspoon powdered ginger
1 teaspoon garlic, finely chopped
1 tablespoon soy sauce
1 tablespoon cornstarch
1 package dumpling wrappers (24 wrappers per package)

Ingredients for Dipping Sauce
¼ cup soy sauce
2 tablespoons white vinegar

Instructions:

1. To make your filling, place cabbage, scallions, pork, ginger, garlic, soy sauce, and cornstarch in a large mixing bowl. Mix well.
2. Fill a small bowl with water.
3. Lay out a dumpling wrapper. Place a teaspoon of filling in the center of the wrapper. Dip your fingers in the water and wet the inside edge of the wrapper. Fold the wrapper into a half circle and pinch the edges together to seal. Repeat with the remaining wrappers and filling.
4. Half fill a three-quart pot with water and bring to a boil. With the help of **an adult**, add 6-10 dumplings. Don't make the pot too crowded! After the water boils again, cook for five minutes, stirring so the dumplings don't stick together. Remove dumplings with a slotted spoon and drain, then place in a serving dish.
5. Repeat step 4 until all the dumplings are cooked. (For crispier dumplings, saute in a pan in vegetable oil for a few minutes).
6. To make dipping sauce, mix the soy sauce and vinegar together.
7. Serve your dumplings with bowls of dipping sauce. Makes about 24 dumplings.

Wonton Soup

Wontons are small dumplings, usually filled with pork. You can eat them by themselves or add them to chicken broth to make this tasty soup.

Ingredients:

8   ounces ground pork
1   tablespoon finely chopped scallions
1   egg, beaten
1   tablespoon soy sauce
1   tablespoon sugar
1   tablespoon water
1   package wonton wrappers (24 per package)
4   cups chicken or vegetable broth

Instructions:

1. Mix pork, scallions, egg, soy sauce, sugar, and water.
2. Lay out wonton wrappers. Put one teaspoon of the pork mixture in the center of each wrapper. Wet your fingers and fold wontons into triangles, pressing the edges together to seal in the filling.
3. Bring a large pot of water to a boil. With the help of **an adult**, drop in a few wontons at a time. Cook over medium heat for 10 minutes. The wontons will float to the top when they are cooked.
4. In a separate pot, bring broth to a boil.
5. Transfer the cooked wontons to the broth with a slotted spoon and cook for one more minute.
6. Pour soup into bowls and serve. Serves 4 people.

Egg Rolls

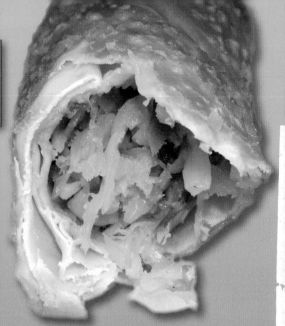

An egg roll is an appetizer that was originally served in East Asia. It has spread throughout the world as a staple of Asian cuisine. Many Asian countries claim to have invented the dish, and variations of the egg roll exist in multiple Asian cuisines.

Ingredients:

½ pound ground pork
¾ pound bagged coleslaw mix
1 cup chopped fresh mushrooms
1 teaspoon chopped garlic
½ teaspoon ground ginger
3 tablespoons soy sauce
½ cup vegetable oil
   Egg roll wrappers

Instructions:

1. With the help of **an adult**, brown the pork in a skillet for a few minutes, then drain off the fat.
2. Add coleslaw mix, mushrooms, garlic, and ginger to the skillet.
3. Stir-fry everything until vegetables are tender.
4. Drain liquid from pan and stir in soy sauce.
5. Spoon about 2 tablespoons of the mixture onto each egg roll wrapper, spreading the mixture evenly.
6. Brush the edges of each wrapper with water to seal them.
7. Roll up the wrappers into tubes.
8. Fry the egg rolls in vegetable oil in the skillet until brown.
9. Drain egg rolls on paper towels to absorb the grease. Serves 4-6.

Almond Cookies

People in China do not have as much of a sweet tooth as people do in the United States. Dessert in China is usually a bowl of fresh fruit. Although cookies are sometimes eaten, they are not the sugary-sweet or chocolate products popular in the United States. Instead, Chinese people prefer lighter cookies, often made with fresh nuts or fruit. Almond cookies are a very popular dessert in China, and make a great afternoon snack as well.

Ingredients:

2   cups all-purpose flour
1   cup sugar
1   teaspoon baking soda
¼   teaspoon salt
2   eggs
2   tablespoons milk
1   tablespoon almond extract
½   cup (1 stick) melted butter
    vegetable shortening, or more butter
¼   cup almonds, sliced in half

1. Mix flour, sugar, baking soda, and salt in a bowl.
2. Crack eggs into a separate small bowl and beat with a fork. Add milk and almond extract and mix well.
3. Pour the melted butter into the flour mixture.
4. Pour the egg mixture into the flour mixture. Stir until you have a soft dough.
5. Grease cookie sheets with vegetable shortening or more butter.
6. Shape dough into small balls and place on the cookie sheets about 1 to 2 inches apart. Make sure balls are not touching each other, because they will spread out as they cook.
7. Use your thumb to make a dent in the top of each ball. Press one almond into each dent.
8. Preheat oven to 375°F. Ask **an adult** to place cookie sheets in oven and bake for 15-20 minutes, or until cookies are light brown.
9. Using oven mitts, remove cookies and place on a rack to cool. Makes 12-15 cookies.

Tea

Tea has been grown in China for centuries. This beverage is incredibly healthy and has been shown to reduce the risk of cancer, heart disease, and other serious illnesses. Tea comes in different varieties, including black, green, and white, depending on how it is processed. You can make tea by placing a tea bag into a cup of boiling water, or you can try this recipe for a more traditional Chinese tea.

Ingredients:

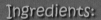

4 teaspoons of loose tea
4 cups of water

Instructions:

Work with **an adult** for this recipe.
1. Fill a teakettle with water and bring it to a boil.
2. Take a small amount of the boiling water and rinse out the teapot to warm and clean it.
3. Measure the loose tea into the pot.
4. Pour the boiling water into the teapot. Cover and let stand for several minutes for the tea to brew. The longer you let the tea brew, the darker and stronger it will be.
5. Pour tea into cups and serve. Serves 4 people.

Sweet Rice Balls

Sweet rice balls served in soup are a popular treat at the Chinese Lantern Festival, which is celebrated during the first full moon of the new year and officially welcomes spring. The rice balls are a symbol of happiness and family togetherness.

Ingredients for Rice Balls
1 cup sweet rice flour
1 tablespoon corn oil
½ cup water

Ingredients for Soup
4 cups water
1 cup sugar
1 teaspoon almond extract

Instructions for Making Rice Balls
1. Pour the rice flour into a large mixing bowl.
2. With the help of **an adult**, bring the water to a boil. Mix oil into the water and pour the mixture slowly into the rice flour, stirring with a wooden spoon as you do so. The mixture will form a dough.
3. Let the dough cool. Then place it on a floured cutting board and knead it until the dough is smooth.
4. Roll the dough into a long log.
5. Cut the roll into small pieces and roll each piece into a ball. Place each ball on a cookie sheet that has been dusted with rice flour. Set the balls aside while you make the soup.

Instructions for Making Soup
1. With **an adult's** help, boil the water and sugar in a large pot. Make sure the sugar is fully dissolved. Then add the rice balls and bring the soup to a boil again. Reduce heat to low and simmer for 8-10 minutes. The rice balls will float to the surface when they are ready.
2. Stir in almond extract.
3. Ladle soup and rice balls into bowls and serve. Serves 4 people.

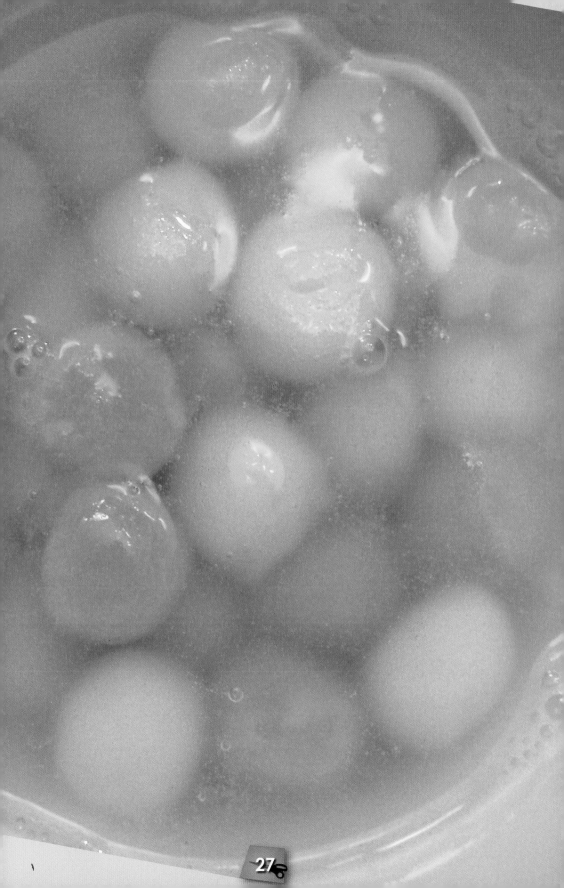

Moon Cakes

The Autumn Moon Festival is the biggest celebration of the fall. This festival honors the moon, so people enjoy special moon cakes (round cakes shaped like the full moon). Moon cakes can have many different fillings, both sweet and salty, such as fruit, beans, or meat. This recipe uses sweet fruits.

Ingredients for Cakes
¾ cup butter
4 cups all-purpose flour
¾ cup powdered milk
1 teaspoon salt
1 tablespoon baking powder
1 cup sugar
3 eggs
1 teaspoon vanilla extract

Ingredients for Filling
1 cup fruit preserves (choose your favorite flavor)
½ cup chopped walnuts
½ teaspoon ground cinnamon

Instructions:

1. Melt butter over low heat and let cool.
2. Sift together flour, powdered milk, salt, and baking powder in a large bowl.
3. In another large bowl, mix eggs and sugar with an electric mixer for about 2 minutes or until smooth. Add butter, vanilla, and the flour mixture. Mix on low speed for about 2 minutes or until it makes a sticky dough.
4. Sprinkle flour on a cutting board and on your hands. Place dough onto the cutting board and knead for about 30 seconds.
5. Shape dough into a log. Wrap in plastic wrap and refrigerate for about 30 minutes.
6. To make the filling, combine preserves, walnuts, and cinnamon in a bowl and set aside.
7. Preheat oven to 375°F. Place 24 foil baking cups or 24 metal moon cake molds onto cookie sheets.
8. Remove dough from the refrigerator and cut into ½-inch slices. Flatten slightly so you can roll the dough around the filling.
9. Place one teaspoon of filling in the center of each circle. Lift the edges of the dough over the filling and pinch closed. Shape the dough to fit into the cupcake cups or molds.
10. With the help of **an adult**, bake your cakes in the oven for 25 minutes, or until they are brown on top.
11. Using oven mitts, have **the adult** lift the cakes out of the oven and onto a cooling rack.
12. Remove the foil cups or molds and serve. Makes 24 cakes.

Introduction
Chinese Crafts

Chinese art usually includes delicate illustrations, sculpture, and pottery, with many intricate details and bright colors. Natural subjects are a favorite in Chinese art, and you will see many images of animals, flowers, and scenes from nature. Although we have included several patterns and examples of Chinese art in this book, you can find many more online or in books at your school or local library. See On the Internet on page 61 for some online resources.

Many of the arts and crafts materials required for these projects are common household items. Others can be purchased at arts and crafts stores. The Internet is also a good source for buying art materials.

A Chinese painting: Gathering mulberry leaves

Cool Secrets for Creating Great Crafts

Read through the instructions—all the way—before you start. This tip can be hard to follow, because you might be so eager to start, you'll dive right in. That's the right spirit! But read all the way through anyway. You'll be glad you did.

Gather all your materials first. A missing item might make you stop halfway through, and then you won't feel like finishing.

Protect your work surface. Lay down newspaper or a plastic tablecloth. (This is a step your parents will be glad you took!) Wear old clothes.

Be creative. You might think of a great new step to add or a twist that gives the craft your personal touch. While you're at it, learn from your mistakes. Try a craft a few times to get it right. Your craft doesn't have to look like the one in the picture to be great.

Be careful. When the instructions tell you to get help from an adult, get help from an adult!

Clean up right away. It's much easier to clean paintbrushes, wipe down surfaces, and wash tools (including your hands) while the mess is fresh. Plus, when you ask for permission to start a new project, you can remind your parents that you cleaned up last time.

You could also ask your parents to join you. Crafts are even more fun when someone does them with you.

As you go about your everyday activities, save things that might be good for your projects. Shoeboxes, toilet paper rolls, ribbon and tissue paper from a gift—these can all be used to make crafts that you'll enjoy keeping or giving to friends and family.

The final secret? Have fun! If you don't enjoy it, there's no point in crafting.

Tangrams

The tangram is an ancient Chinese puzzle made out of a square cut into seven pieces. People use the pieces to create different pictures, such as a cat, boat, bird, rabbit, or anything else you can imagine!

Materials:

Sturdy paper, such as card stock
Pencil
Ruler
Scissors

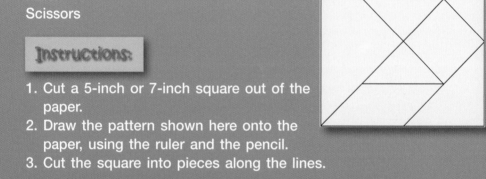

Instructions:

1. Cut a 5-inch or 7-inch square out of the paper.
2. Draw the pattern shown here onto the paper, using the ruler and the pencil.
3. Cut the square into pieces along the lines.

4. Use all seven pieces of your tangram to create pictures. Challenge your friends to match your pictures or create their own patterns. Here are some ideas for you and your friends to try:

Paper Cutouts

Chinese people often use paper cutouts to decorate their homes. They cut out pictures of animals, flowers, or just pretty designs and tape them to windows and doors to brighten up the room. You can make some cutouts of your own and hang them to decorate your room or your locker at school.

Materials:

Construction paper in two
    different colors (it's best to use
    colors that contrast well, such
    as a dark color and a light
    color)
Pencil
Scissors
Glue

Instructions:

1. Draw or trace your picture onto a piece of construction paper.

2. Cut out the pattern.
3. Glue the cutout onto the other piece of construction paper until the whole cutout is pasted down.

Please trace.
DO NOT cut
this book.

Fireworks

Fireworks were invented in China thousands of years ago and are an important part of many holiday celebrations. Although it is much too dangerous to make your own fireworks, you can create colorful fireworks pictures.

Materials:

Black or dark blue construction paper
Acrylic paint in different colors
Small paintbrush
Glitter
Old newspapers

Instructions:

1. Spread the old newspapers on the table where you are going to work.
2. Paint colorful designs on the construction paper. Use as many different colors as you want.
3. Sprinkle glitter into the paint while it is still wet.
4. Allow paint to dry. Shake extra glitter off of the paper.

Kites

Kites were first used in China as far back as 770 BCE. Today, kites come in many shapes and sizes. If you walk through parks in Chinese cities, you will often see people flying kites. Here's how to make your own simple kite to fly on a windy day.

Materials:

Butcher paper or gift-wrapping paper, about 18 inches by 30 inches
Scissors
Pencil
Markers
2 18-inch dowels, each ⅛-inch thick
Packing tape
Pin
Ball of thin string
Crepe-paper streamers
Long stick or cardboard tube
Metal ring (a ring from a keychain will work)

Instructions:

1. Cut your paper into a large hexagon.
2. Decorate your paper with markers. You can draw a picture or a design—whatever you like! Tape streamers to the edge of the kite.
3. Turn the paper over and tape the dowels onto the back. The dowels should go up and down, from the top left to bottom left, and top right to bottom right. The outer points do not need support.
4. Put a piece of tape on each point on the kite. Use the pin to punch two holes through each point.
5. Cut a piece of string about 4 feet long. Knot the ends of the string through the holes. Put another piece of tape over the back of the holes to keep the string in place.

6. Wind the rest of the string around a stick or cardboard tube. Tie the free end to the middle of the string attached to your kite.

7. Take your kite outside to fly on a day with a steady breeze. To get started, run into the wind with your kite held up in the air. You can control the kite by holding onto the string.

Dragon Boats

Ancient Chinese people worshiped a water dragon god and began celebrating festivals in the dragon's honor about 2,500 years ago. Dragon boat races became an important part of these celebrations. You can build your own dragon boat out of paper and hold races with your friends.

Materials:

2 pieces of red construction paper
Pencil
Scissors
Markers
2 pieces of clear contact paper
Masking tape or stapler
Foam rubber strip, about 2 inches in diameter and 9 inches long
Quarter

Instructions:

1. Use the pencil to draw a boat with a dragon's head and tail on one piece of paper.

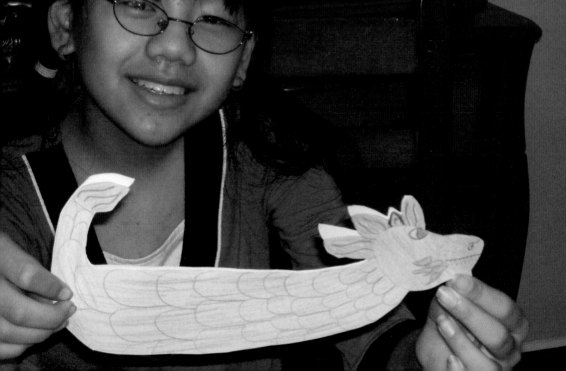

2. Place both pieces of paper together and cut through them so that you have two identical dragon boat shapes.
3. Decorate both dragon boat shapes with markers.
4. Cover each piece of paper with contact paper.
5. Tape or staple the heads and tails of the dragon shapes together to make one boat. Be sure to leave space at the bottom to insert the piece of foam rubber.
6. Tape the quarter to the back end of the foam rubber to balance your boat.
7. Slip the foam rubber between the two sides of the boat and tape into place.
8. Your boat will float in a bathtub or any other large tub of water. Move your hands through the water to create waves to make the boat travel. Have a race with your friends!

CLOTH AND CLAY CRAFTS
Scented Bag

The plum blossom is the national flower of China and the first flower to bloom in the spring. An old-fashioned Chinese tradition says that carrying a bag of scented flower petals will keep away evil spirits. It's also nice to smell sweet flowers any time! Here's a simple scented bag you can make and carry with you.

Materials:

6-inch x 9-inch piece of cloth in a bright color or pattern
Needle and thread
Potpourri or scented flower petals
Piece of colorful yarn

Instructions:

1. Fold the cloth in half with the wrong side facing out.
2. Use the needle and thread to sew two sides of the cloth closed. Leave one end open to create a bag.
3. Turn the bag right side out so that the seams are inside the bag.
4. Fill the bag with potpourri or flower petals.
5. Tie the bag closed with the piece of yarn.

Dough Clay Figures

Pandas are found in the wild in just one country: China! They live in forests and only eat a plant called bamboo. However, pandas are endangered and very few still live in the wild. Instead, most of China's pandas live on preserves where they are carefully bred to increase the population. China has entrusted several pandas with other countries, including the United States, as a gesture of friendship.

You can use flour, water, and salt to make a type of clay, and use it to make your own panda.

Materials:

Old newspapers
Bowl
1 cup cold water
1 cup salt
2 teaspoons vegetable oil
2 cups all-purpose flour
2 tablespoons cornstarch
Wet paper towel
Small paintbrush
Black and white tempera or acrylic paints
White glue

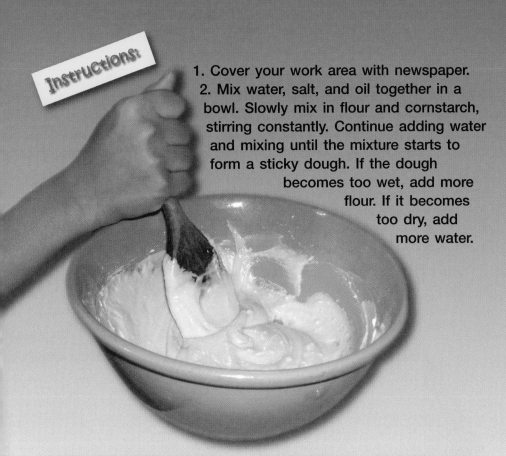

1. Cover your work area with newspaper.
2. Mix water, salt, and oil together in a bowl. Slowly mix in flour and cornstarch, stirring constantly. Continue adding water and mixing until the mixture starts to form a sticky dough. If the dough becomes too wet, add more flour. If it becomes too dry, add more water.

3. Take the dough out of the bowl and knead it with both hands until it is flexible and easy to work with.

4. Break off a piece of dough and cover the rest of the dough with a wet paper towel until you need it.

5. Roll some dough into a ball about 1¾ inches across for the body. Roll a smaller ball to make the head. Roll small balls to make the ears and legs. Roll two balls into small sausage shapes for the arms.

6. Use your finger to make a small dent on the body where the other pieces will be attached. Dip your finger in water and wet both places. Then join the pieces together to make your panda.

7. Let your panda dry for about two days. If you want it to dry faster, **ask an adult** to put it on a cookie sheet and place the figure in the oven for about three hours at 250°F. Allow the figure to cool completely after the adult takes it out of the oven.

8. To decorate your panda, paint it white. Let the paint dry. Then paint the arms, legs, ears, eyes, and nose black.

9. Let your panda dry for a few days. When it is completely dry, cover it with two coats of white glue to preserve the figure and keep it from getting sticky.

Holiday Crafts

Chinese New Year is the biggest holiday in China. Unlike the Western calendar, the Chinese calendar is determined by phases of the moon. That means that Chinese New Year can fall anytime between late January and the middle of February.

Each year of the Chinese calendar is represented by a different animal. For example, 2010 is the Year of the Tiger. The Chinese calendar works on a twelve-year cycle, with twelve animals in each cycle. These animals are the rat, ox, tiger, rabbit, dragon, snake, horse, sheep, monkey, rooster, dog, and pig. Different qualities are given to people based on the year in which they were born. For example, someone born in the year of the horse would be cheerful and popular.

There are several different legends that explain why these particular twelve animals make up the zodiac. One legend says that the animals raced across the river to determine what order they would be in the calendar. The rat rode across on the ox's back and jumped off at the last minute to win the race. The pig was lazy and didn't make much effort, so he finished last. Another legend states that the gods summoned all the animals for a meeting, but only twelve animals bothered to show up. To thank them, the gods assigned a year on the calendar to each of those twelve animals.

Red Lanterns

Gung Hay Fat Choy! means "Happy New Year" in Chinese. During the New Year, people gather for parades. They set off firecrackers and make lots of noise to scare away evil spirits. They also give children gifts in red envelopes. Red is a lucky color in China. You will see many red lanterns hung as decorations at New Year celebrations. These decorations are easy and fun to make.

Materials:

Red construction paper
Pencil
Scissors
Stapler, tape, or glue

Instructions:

1. Fold a piece of construction paper in half to make a long rectangle.
2. Draw a line about one inch from the unfolded edge.
3. Cut slits all along the paper along the fold line, about ½ inch apart. Cut up to the line you drew in step #2, making sure not to cut all the way through the paper.
4. Unfold the paper and glue, staple, or tape the short edges together to make your lantern.
5. Cut a strip of paper 6 inches long by ½ inch wide. Glue, staple, or tape the strip across the top of the lantern to make a handle.

Dragon Toy

Dragon and lion parades are a tradition on New Year's Day. These animals are powerful symbols of strength and good luck. Crowds watch as two or more people wear a giant dragon or lion costume and dance and parade through the streets. You can make a toy version of the dancing dragon.

Materials:

Construction paper
Long red piece of paper (you can glue two pieces of construction
    paper together or use red gift-wrapping paper)
Scissors
Markers
Glue
Tape
2 chopsticks or wooden barbecue skewers
Glitter
Feathers

Instructions:

1. Draw the head and tail of a dragon on a piece of paper. The head should be about six inches long and the tail about eight inches long.
2. Cut out the head and tail and decorate them with the markers, glitter, and feathers.
3. Fold the red piece of paper up like an accordion to make the dragon's body.

4. Glue the dragon's head to one end of the red piece of paper. Glue the dragon's tail to the other end.
5. Tape one chopstick or skewer to the head and the other to the tail to hold up your dragon.

Paper Firecracker

According to Chinese tradition, making noise chases away evil spirits, so people make plenty of noise to start the New Year off in a good way! You will often hear firecrackers at New Year's parades and celebrations. You can make safe paper firecrackers filled with candy following these simple instructions.

Materials:

Empty toilet paper tube
Red tissue paper
Yarn
Plastic wrap
Small pieces of candy, about one handful per firecracker
Tape
Black and colored markers

1. Wrap the candy in the plastic wrap. Tie the bundle closed with a piece of yarn, leaving about 6 inches of yarn hanging from the knot.
2. Place the wrapped candy inside the toilet paper tube, letting the yarn hang out.
3. Wrap the tube in the tissue paper, making sure that the yarn hangs out of the top. Tuck the paper inside the bottom of the tube and tape it in place to close.
4. Twist the paper at the top of the firecracker around the loose ends of yarn. Wrap a strip of tape around the yarn to hold everything in place. This will be the fuse for your firecracker.
5. Decorate the firecracker by drawing Chinese characters or pictures on the outside.
6. To "set off" your firecrackers, pull on the fuse to tear the tissue and pull out the candy. Although this won't explode like a firecracker, it will pop open to reveal a tasty treat inside!

Further Reading

Books

Bledsoe, Karen E. *Chinese New Year Crafts*. Berkeley Heights, NJ: Enslow Elementary, 2005.

Fauchild, Nick. *Wrap-n-Bake Egg Rolls and Other Chinese Dishes*. Minneapolis: Picture Window Books, 2009.

Kramer, Lance. *Great Ancient China Projects You Can Build Yourself*. White River Junction, VT: Nomad Press, 2008.

Lee, Frances. *Fun with Chinese Cooking*. New York: PowerKids Press, 2010.

———. *The Young Chef's Chinese Cookbook*. St. Catharines, Ontario: Crabtree Publishing, 2001.

Locricchio, Matthew. *The Cooking of China*. New York: Benchmark Books, 2002.

McGee, Randel. *Paper Crafts for Chinese New Year*. Berkeley Heights, NJ: Enslow Elementary, 2008.

Sheen, Barbara. *Foods of China*. Farmington Hills, MI: KidHaven Press, 2006.

Simonds, Nina, and Leslie Swartz. *Moonbeams, Dumplings and Dragon Boats*. New York: Harcourt Books, 2002.

Thompson, Stuart, and Angela Dennington. *Chinese Festivals Cookbook*. Austin, TX: Raintree Steck-Vaughn, 2001.

Yu, Ling. *Cooking the Chinese Way*. Minneapolis: Lerner Publications Company, 2002.

Works Consulted

Best Recipes: Chinese Favorites. Lincolnwood, IL: Publications International, Ltd., 2010.

Chang, Norma. *My Students' Favorite Chinese Recipes*. Wappingers Falls, NY: 2001.

Kwong, Kylie. *Simple Chinese Cooking*. New York: Viking, 2006.

Lauret Parkinson, Rhonda. *The Everything Chinese Cookbook*. Avon, MA: Adams Media Corporation, 2003.

Further Reading

Liang, Lucille. *Dim Sum Made Easy*. New York: Sterling Publishing, 2006.

Moey, S.C. *Chinese Feasts and Festivals: A Cookbook*. Singapore: Periplus Editions, 2006.

Temko, Florence. *Traditional Crafts from China*. Minneapolis: Lerner Publications Company, 2001.

On the Internet

Ancient Chinese Art
http://www.historyforkids.org/learn/china/art

Asia Art
http://www.asia-art.net

Chinese Food Recipes
http://www.chinesefood-recipes.com

Chinese New Year Recipes
http://chinesefood.about.com/od/chinesenewyear/tp/easy_recipes.htm

Chinese Recipes
http://www.recipezaar.com/recipes/chinese

Chinese Zodiac Page
http://www.c-c-c.org/chineseculture/zodiac/zodiac.html

Easy Chinese Recipes
http://familyfun.go.com/recipes/chinese-cook-in-714603

Enchanted Learning
http://www.enchantedlearning.com/crafts/chinesenewyear/

A Trip to a Chinese Wet Market
http://www.squidoo.com/chinese-wet-market

Glossary

beat (BEET)—To mix quickly with a fork or electric mixer.

chopsticks (CHOP-stiks)—Thin wooden sticks used for eating.

colander (KAHL-un-dur)—A metal bowl with holes, used to drain water from food.

dumplings (DUMP-lingz)—Small balls of cooked dough, often stuffed with meat or vegetables.

garnish (GAR-nish)—To decorate food with small amounts of fresh herbs or other pieces of colorful foods.

ginger (JIN-jur)—A root that can be chopped or grated and used as a spice.

grease (GREES)—To spread shortening or oil on a pan or cookie sheet to prevent food from sticking to it.

hexagon (HEKS-uh-gon)—A figure with six sides.

hoisin (HOY-sin) **sauce**—A sweet and spicy sauce popular in Chinese cooking.

knead (NEED)—To work dough with your hands to make it smooth.

mein (MAYN)—Noodles.

potpourri (POH-poh-ree)—Dried and scented flowers, leaves, and berries.

saucepan (SOS-pan)—A small cooking pot with a handle.

scallions (SKAL-yunz)—Green onions.

seams (SEEMZ)—Lines where two pieces of material are sewn together.

sift (SIFT)—To put a dry substance, such as flour, through a sieve to get rid of lumps.

skillet (SKIL-ut)—A shallow pan used to fry food.

soy (SOY) **sauce**—A dark, salty sauce made from soybeans.

steamed (STEEMD)—Cooked with moist heat.

stir-fry (STUR-fry)—To cook ingredients quickly over high heat, stirring constantly.

wok (WOK)—A large bowl-shaped skillet.

wontons (WAHN-tahns)—Small dumplings.

Index

ABOUT THE
AUTHOR

Joanne Mattern is the author of many nonfiction books for children. She has profiled many celebrities and sports stars for Mitchell Lane, including the Jonas Brothers, Ashley Tisdale, Peyton Manning, and Michelle Obama, and has written about China and other parts of the world for other publishers. Joanne lives in New York State with her husband, four children (all adopted from China), and an assortment of pets.